The Crea Adam

Seven Guided Reflections from Genesis

David Runcorn

Director of Pastoral Studies and Tutor in Spirituality,
Trinity Theological College, Bristol

GROVE BOOKS LIMITED
RIDLEY HALL RD CAMBRIDGE CB3 9HU

Contents

Introducing the Sculpture and the Meditations 3

1. On Praying with Open Eyes 6

2. The Unfinished Creation 9

3. The Fullness of Time 12

4. The Search for Belonging 15

5. The Wound of Becoming 18

6. The Cost of Creating 20

7. Blessing and Hallowing 23

Acknowledgements

Grateful thanks to Graham Pigott and to my wife Jackie Searle for their comments on the emerging text of this booklet. And to participants in various conferences, workshops and Quiet Days whose enthusiasm and openness has brought these stories to life again.

Dedication

To my parents, Dennis and Heather Runcorn,
for their love in my beginning;
their encouragement in all my becoming;
and who themselves
have never stopped
becoming.

Cover Photograph

I obtained this photograph in France some years ago and have had difficulty trying to trace a copyright holder, if such exists. I will continue the search and I am grateful for any assistance.

First Impression February 2001
ISSN 0262-799X
ISBN 1 85174 456 8

Introducing the Sculpture and the Meditations

In the Beginning

The sculpture in the picture on the inside cover comes from Chartres Cathedral. It was probably carved between 1200–1250. It is found at the apex of one of the arches under the North Portical. If you hold the picture directly above your head and look straight up at it that gives you the perspective. But it is less than a metre long and surrounded by the host of other sculpted scenes from biblical life that cover that magnificent building.

A photo of this sculpture has travelled with me for nearly ten years. It has found itself on the walls of a variety of homes and studies where my human story has been unfolding.

Hanging there, just above the joys and pains of the daily round, it has become a friend. I have only slowly realized how much, almost unnoticed, it has encouraged, challenged, interpreted and shaped my living and praying. In the process it has made me contemplate the over-familiar story of human creation through fresh eyes and I have found myself asking unexpected questions about what it all means.

In recent years I have increasingly used this picture for leading prayer groups and quiet days and, in the context of my present job, as a way of exploring the mystery of Christian vocation and ministry formation.

Praying and Contemplating the Creation Stories

The creation stories are arguably among the most misused and abused passages of Scripture. In some quarters they have been forced into the front line as a test of orthodoxy, to defend 'The Faith' against science, evolution and all things 'liberal,' history against myth. They have also been read as factual explanations for the origin of evil, sin, death or even the problem of sex. As a result we have lost the imagination of the storyteller and the freedom to pray with what we read. This booklet aims to open up a contemplative reading of these Scriptures.

Some Background

There are two stories of creation in Genesis. Like all stories they have evolved and been shaped in the telling, but they are thought to have found their significant biblical voice at two very contrasting times in the life of God's people.

The first story (Gen 1–2.4) is thought to have emerged among the exiled people in Babylon, in the 6th century BC. This was not just national catastrophe. It was a theological disaster. The Temple was destroyed. God appeared to have been defeated. How could they sing the Lord's song in a strange land (Ps 137)?

This is a pastoral story to build up the hope, the identity and the prayers of God's people in the face of disaster and exile. It affirms that God can still create out of the formless void into which life has collapsed (Gen 1.1). It steadily affirms

God's purpose and ordering of the world. It finally affirms humanity as the crown of creation, bearing the very image of God. All this is probably over-familiar to us. Imagine this story told, sung, prayed among a shanty town of refugees from a far country, disinherited, disenfranchised, powerless of themselves to remake their lives. This is their story. This is their God. As we, in our turn, hear this story, how does it speak to our world and its concerns?

The second creation story (Gen 2.4–3.24) probably originates from an earlier period of Israel's history—in the tenth century royal court of King Solomon. It was a time of ascendant international prestige, the sophisticated high point of culture, knowledge, progress and human potential. To such a people a very different story is told. Humanity is not the final, glorious pinnacle of creation but is created first—and out of the dust. This is a story about boundary, knowledge and vocation and warns against pride and trespass of what belongs to God alone.

They now stand in reverse of their historic order. The first story says to humanity living with chaos and exile—'this is still the glory of our vocation in God's creation.' The second story is a commentary on the first and warns—'and these are the challenges, opportunities and perils that face us as we seek to be faithful to this vocation.'

adam—The 'Earth Creature'

This booklet is not a systematic prayer commentary on the creation stories. All the meditations focus on the point of *adam's* emerging into life under the creative hands of God. This has three implications.

First, because I have used this sculpture as my starting point, there are parts of the creation stories I have not explored directly. The themes in the meditations are part of a much greater whole. This is one of a number of sculptures of God and humanity. They all show different stages of the creation story. (I am still searching for a sculpture of God breathing life into the human's nostrils).

Secondly, we are invited by the sculptor to contemplate *adam* before what we traditionally call 'The Fall.' This means that although the meditations include reflection on the experience of sin and fallenness (and it is impossible not to), the primary interest is in exploring the vocation to be a human being.

Thirdly, the scene in this sculpture is prior to the gift of Eve. The name *adam* translates 'earth creature,' being closely related to the word *adamah* meaning 'earth.' The common translation 'man' is unhelpful because at this point in creation 'man' and 'woman' have not been physically or sexually differentiated. To use the name 'earth creature' feels too inhuman.

So to try to express the inclusiveness of being created human in this sculpture I henceforth use the name *adam* in italics and lower case.

Using These Meditations

Each meditation focuses on one aspect of creation as suggested by the sculpture. The starting point of each meditation arises out of a personal response to what I have seen there as I have reflected upon it. Someone once said, 'The artist makes a statement; the viewer completes it.' So my perceptions arise out this engagement and are offered to help you explore and be enriched by your own—sensitive to the Spirit's prompting in this process.

So these meditations, which are for individual or group use, offer a place of shared reflection, prayer and exploration—with the Bible story, the sculpture, the sculptor, the author of this booklet—and whoever uses it to read and to pray.

Preparation

Reading the original. Before starting these meditations, it is important to read the creation stories in Genesis. Over-familiarity may be a problem here. Reading aloud, or with a different Bible translation, can restore an element of freshness or surprise to what we read.

Before you begin a meditation start by taking time to relax, to unwind from what-ever activities you bring to this prayer time. The simplest way is to listen to, and rest in, the rhythm of your own breathing. Only then will you begin to have space to receive what the sculpture is offering—and to make your own responses to it.

The shape of the meditations. Each meditation follows the same outline and con-cludes with a variety of suggestions for reflection, praying and creative response to the theme.

- **Seeing**. Each meditation starts by briefly suggesting one insight or feature of the sculpture. It is important to take time to 'see' and not assume that we 'know' the picture well enough. This is followed by a time of silent 'gazing,' I suggest for about 10 minutes.
- **Connecting** and **Reflecting**. These sections offer biblical and personal points of connection and discussion around the theme. They are starters and make no claim to be exhaustive. Members of a group may be encouraged to offer their own response to the theme and the sculpture, for about 15 minutes, with-out any discussion, just listening to each other.
- **Responding**. These are some quotations, prayers and creative suggestions for exploring the themes further. Paper, paints and charcoal or even clay could be provided. We are using a sculpture to contemplate Scripture. As the sculptor once used his senses—touch, feel, imagination, texture—as a means to medi-tate on Scripture, alone or in a group, you are invited to do the same. Perhaps each meditation could include a 'free time' for using paint, colours or clay to explore the themes 'hands on.'

  There can be a barrier to overcome at this point. Many of us have hang ups about 'doing art.' We are paralysed by the need for it to be 'good.' In medita-tion the end product is not the priority. The key is having time to explore and experiment. Our senses have their own contribution to make if they are given time and space. They will be enriching our praying. I suggest 30 minutes for this section.
- **Closing**. This time may include sharing and praying as a group. The time should conclude, as it began, with some time just gazing at the sculpture.

1

On Praying with Open Eyes

'And God *saw* that it was good.' (Genesis 1.18)

Seeing
We start by just looking at the picture.

> The first demand any work of art makes of upon us is surrender.
> Look. Listen. Receive.
> Get yourself out of the way.   (C S Lewis)

The sculpture is going to accompany us through these meditations. We must first take time to get to know it. Just look at it. Do not be distracted by ideas or feelings about it. Just look at it. We will be tempted to drawing conclusions too quickly about what we see.

Resist the need to 'explain' or 'understand' what we are looking at. We are not looking for what we can get out of it, or for what it 'says' to us.

Just look at it.

Take 10 minutes for this. (If you get restless take a break and then come back and look again.)

Ask for grace to gaze—to 'behold.' 'Lord, open my eyes to see.'

When you have taken time to look, ask yourself:
What are your first thoughts and feelings as you look at this sculpture?
Does this scene remind you of other Bible stories?
Who do you most identify with in this sculpture?
Would the picture be different if you were in it either as forming or being formed? If so in what way?

Connecting
After each stage in the creation story we read that God stopped and looked. God 'saw.' We are not told he thought or he felt. He *saw*. Is this important? Or was he just taking a break? In some cultures of the world to truly 'see' someone or something is very significant. Seeing gives life. Western patterns of greeting generally ask us to identify or declare ourselves—'*How are you?*' But in parts of Africa, for example, the greeting is an affirmation not a question. 'I see you.' And in that seeing, a gift of recognition, of honour and worth is bestowed. In the Bible this is where our sense of identity begins—in our recognition by another—and supremely by God. Creation is truly given to itself in the moment it is recognized.

As God greets our emerging world—'I see you'—he celebrates it—'it is good.'

The word 'good' means more than 'well made' or 'without fault.' It would be better translated with words like 'lovely,' 'pleasing,' 'beautiful,' 'enriching.'

Verse after verse carries this refrain, 'and God saw.' It finally builds up to his slow, wide, delighted gaze across all creation when we read: 'And God saw *everything* that he had made—and indeed, it was *very* good.' (Genesis 1.31)

Reflecting

Chartres Cathedral was built for a world before most people could read and long before printing presses. For them, knowing their Bibles was a matter of careful *seeing*, rather than careful reading. They 'read' the Bible from the stained glass windows. They 'told' its stories from the stone friezes that covered the walls with scenes of biblical and medieval life, woven together with sumptuous vitality.

This world of the 'visual word' has much in common with our own where communication is increasingly through sight, and verbal communication is reduced to link commentary or sound bites.

By contrast, the experience of church for many people remains highly verbal and conceptual rather than visual. We are still influenced by Christian traditions that regard the human senses of sight, hearing, smell, touch with suspicion—as too subjective and unreliable. Rational thought is considered superior and a more reliable means of expressing something and defining its meaning.

But the creation began with seeing. And it still does.

> Seeing comes before words. The child looks and recognizes before it can speak. But there is another sense in which seeing comes before words. It is seeing which establishes our place in the surrounding world. The relation between what we see and what we know is never settled…this seeing comes before words and can never be quite covered by them.   (Peter Berger)

In this world, open eyes are no guarantee of clear sight. We should not be surprised that, of all his healing miracles, blindness to sight is the one Jesus continually uses to teach and warn about our central human predicament. This a world of distorted vision. True seeing does not come naturally. It is a gift and we must learn to use it well.

Jesus once said, 'I came into this world for judgment so that those who do not see may see and those who do see may become blind.' Some of the Pharisees near him heard this and said, 'Surely we are not blind are we?' Jesus said to them, 'If you were blind, you would not have sin. But now that you say, "We see" your sin remains' (John 9.40–1). On another occasion it was the physically blind man, Bartimaeus, who recognized his need when he heard that Jesus was nearby. 'Then Jesus said to him, "What do you want me to do for you?" The blind man said to him, "Lord I want to receive my sight"' (Mark 10.46ff).

Responding

Return to the picture for a few moments in silence.

How does God 'see'? It may be the effect of weathering on this sculpture but God's eyes seem to be shut, or even blind. He appears to be 'seeing' through his hands. Yet *everything* about his figure is quietly attentive. His whole being appears to be watchfully attentive to *adam* and his head is inclined towards him.

Seeing involves the whole of our being. It is a contemplative vocation.

You might explore this by spending some time shaping clay, painting or drawing with your eyes shut—concentrating on the heart intention of what you long to make.

Imagine God's hands poised above and around your head.

He creates. He pauses. He looks upon you.

He sees—all that he has made.

Let him speak that: 'I see you.'

And he celebrates you—'it is good.' 'You are good.'

Can you hear affirmation like that? Very little in this earthly life prepares us for that kind of joyful recognition and affirmation.

But here it is. More original than any sin and distortion in our lives. The original, earthy, goodness of creation and the God of Creation, who still sees, delights in and is glad about all that he has made.

A Thought?

'Most likely we are still in Eden—only our eyesight has changed.'

(G K Chesterton)

2

The Unfinished Creation

'In the beginning when God *began creating* the heavens and the earth…'

(Genesis 1.1)

Seeing

Look at the sculpture again for a while. What do you see new this time?

adam is only half emerged from the dust of the earth. The sculptor, in his wisdom, has frozen the work of creation at mid point. This human being is incomplete. Unfinished. He is *becoming*. Creation is in process.

adam is halfway between earth and heaven, halfway between being and non-being, halfway between nonexistence and life.

Is it significant that the sculptor should choose to express the work of creation at this moment—in the between-ness of things?

Connecting

'In the beginning…' (Genesis 1.1). At the bottom of this page in your Bible, you will probably find a note explaining that this verse can be translated in different ways.

'In the beginning God created…' can also read, 'In the beginning God *began creating.'*

Both are true. God is the first source of life. Life began in him. But in Psalm 104, for example, this creating gift continues. 'You send forth your spirit and life begins. You (ever) renew the face of the earth' (v 30 *Jerusalem Bible*). In this world we never reach an end to God's creating life and vitality.

This sculpture is a meditation on the second translation. It is a work of creation that is continuing.

A passage in the New Testament takes this insight further:

See what love the Father has given us, that we might be called children of God; and that is what we are…We are God's children now; what we will be has not yet been revealed. What we do know is that when he appears, we will be like him, for we shall see him as he is. (1 John 3.1, 3)

This tells us three things about our life in creation:

Life is Gift   'see what love the Father has given us'
Life is Mystery   'what we will be is not yet revealed'
Life is Promise   'we will be like him'

Before becoming the source of our redemption, Christ is the secret of our creation. 'For in him all things in heaven and earth were created…and in him all things hold together.' (Col 1.16). And the same cosmic, glorified Christ continues to 'sustain all things by his powerful word' (Heb 1.3). Being a human *becomer* means trusting to Jesus the secret of who we are becoming.

Reflecting

This picture hangs on the wall of my study above the considerable clutter and confusion of many unfinished things. I find it very affirming. It gives me permission to be unfinished.

There is no blame in this picture for a human being who has yet to 'get it together.'

Rather, God is willingly involved in our continued emerging into life.

His presence is above, beside and breathed into this *adam* with gentle care and deep concentration.

But this is also an uncomfortable revelation.

The moment we receive the Gift and trust the Promise we also have to enter the Mystery of who we are. It has been said that Christ is the only truly human being; we are human becomers. We are unfinished. But we want to be finished products and with good reason.

This world is not a comfortable place for unfinished, incomplete, undefended people.

We quickly feel our nakedness. We are afraid and we learn to hide.

Out of anxiety and pressure we spend a lot of time carefully trying to look finished!

We never quite lose the fear that those around us will not love and accept us if they saw the places where we are so naked, flawed and incomplete.

Not only does this sculpture affirm our incompleteness—and therefore our becoming—before God. It may also warn of us of the peril of pretending otherwise. Not only is our humanity unfinished and found in mystery—this is a vital part of the gift of being human.

> Human beings need problems more than they need solutions. This is because we are beings with immortal longings and an indelible ideal and we suffer our greatest harm whenever, for a while, success sends us out believing that our ideal has been reached and our longing satisfied.   (John V Taylor)

We are more alive as human *becomers* than as human beings. Our incompleteness is part of the original gift of God in creation.

Responding

Look at the sculpture. Take time for this.

Imagine yourself in the place of *adam*. You are half born, vulnerable, unfinished—emerging somewhere between gift of life and dust of earth—not yet at home in either. What thoughts and feelings do you have?

One way of reflecting on this may be to physically adopt the posture we see in adam *in the sculpture. Kneel by a chair and lean your head on a cushion in prayer.*

Where do you feel your incompleteness most?
Is it more gift or burden to you?

And God? What is God's gift in this picture?
(*adam* may not realize God is there at all...)

Try using colours or charcoal or clay to feel and express this coming into being. If you were the sculptor would you have created this scene differently?

Before praying this closing prayer, it may help to read it through first and (if you are in a group) to respond to it, listening to each other without any discussion.

God leaves me free to be whatever I like.
I can be myself, or not, as I please.
I am at liberty to be real, or to be unreal.
I may be true or false, the choice is mine.
I may wear now one mask and now another,
and never, if I so desire, appear with my own true face.

To work out my own identity in God,
Which the Bible calls 'working out our salvation,'
is a labour that requires sacrifice and anguish, risk and many tears.

I do not know beforehand what the result of this work will be,
the secret of my full identity is hidden in Him.
He alone can make me who I am,
or rather who I will be when at last I fully begin to be.

(Thomas Merton)

3

The Fullness of Time

'And there was evening *and* there was morning, the first day.' (Genesis 1.5)

Seeing
Spend some time looking at the sculpture again.

The scene in this sculpture seems timeless. But perhaps 'time-full' expresses this moment more accurately. There is no apparent urgency to finish the job.

Look at those hands. They seem to have been poised there for ever. The mood is quiet, attentive, unhurried.

Connecting
The whole of this first creation story (Gen 1.1–2.4) is told with a quiet, measured liturgical rhythm. Perhaps it was written to be sung or recited in worship. Each day follows the same cycle: 'Let there be,' 'and there was,' 'and God saw,' 'it was good.'

Although the whole creation story is measured by the passing of seven days, there is no hint that this was all the time God had to spare for the project out of his crowded diary.

No one had to chase him up like an unreliable contractor: 'I know you are very busy but…' God, in this sculpture, has all the time in the world and there seems to be nothing else he would rather do than be creating *adam*.

In the light of this it should come as no surprise that *adam's* first full day in the fullness of creation is a day off! (2.2). In this creation the sabbath rest with God comes *before* work not after it. This is not a reward for work done but an anticipation of life graced. Life is gift, to be entered in trust.

All this feels a long way from our own relationship with time. Despite the ability to do everything in increasingly less time the misery of our age continues to be our lack of it. By contrast this sculpture is enviably at ease with time.

Reflecting
This picture just *is*—capturing and contemplating a divine 'timeless moment.' It is not trying to pick an argument with us, tell us off or 'challenge' us. It is not even interested in what we are thinking at all! But in looking, we are invited to contemplate a quite different way of living in time.

'We tend to think of time longitudinally in all its hectic successiveness—and eternity as endless elongation. We need to enjoy, savour time's weight, depth, thickness and sweetness' (Howard Peskett).

In *Zorba the Greek*, Nicos Kazantzakis tells of a time when he discovered a cocoon in the bark of a tree, just as the butterfly was making a hole in its case and preparing to come out. I waited a little while, but it was too long in appearing and I was impatient. I bent over it and breathed on it to warm it. I warmed it as quickly as I could and the miracle began to happen before my eyes, faster than life. The case opened, the butterfly started slowly crawling out and I shall never forget the horror…when I saw how its wings were folded back and crumpled. The wretched butterfly tried with its whole trembling body to unfold them. Bending over it I tried to help it with my breath. In vain. It needed to be hatched out patiently and the unfolding of its wings would be a gradual process in the sun. Now it was too late. My breath had forced the butterfly to appear, all crumpled, before its time. It struggled desperately and, a few seconds later, died in the palm of my hand.

Many experience the pressures and demands of life as like that hot breath. But a deeper tragedy is when we think that this is what God's breath is like and that this forcing of life is what he requires.

By contrast look at the hands of God in this sculpture.

Pause for a moment by the hands of God.

Chartres Cathedral is nearly 800 years old. Beneath those soaring arches have flowed centuries of wars, plagues, prosperity, poverty, faith, apostasy, hope, despair, laughter and tears.

And where has God been during this time? Over there, high above that side entrance. If you did not know where to look you would easily miss him. And there he keeps his patient vigil. There is no hurrying the hands of God, no distracting the divine intention. This is 'the one thing necessary' (Luke 10.38). He is not trying to make something useful here, but someone for him to delight in and see as good. In that delight we find our purpose.

Responding

How would you complete these sentences?

> I think ………………is a total waste of time.
> My idea of a good time is ………………
> There is never enough time for ………………

What do your answers suggest about your dreams, longings, frustrations and their relationship with time?

Look again at the sculpture.

It suggests other ways of 'being in time.' What does it leave you feeling or wanting to say?

Older clocks often had scenes of life painted around the dial. Draw a large clock face. This is your time. Inside it, draw or paint the scenes that your time-full life might include.

A suggestion:
Do not ask: 'how should I be spending my time?' Ask instead, 'who am I spending my time becoming?'

I will not glorify God in my life by doing something—but by becoming someone.

Being practical and accepting our limits:
'Find enough time to pray, enough time to sleep, then do what you can'

(Austin Farrer)

You might like to write your own prayer about time and becoming. Or make use of these.

We live in the fullness of time.
Every moment is God's own good time, his *kairos*.*
The whole thing boils down to giving ourselves in prayer a chance
to realize that we have what we seek.
We don't have to rush after it.
It is there all the time.
And if we give it time it will make itself known to us.

(Thomas Merton)

A Prayer to the Lord of my Time
(from one who has often been in a hurry)

Lord of the years, of months and weeks and days, of all times and seasons,
Whose wonderfully exact providence grants to all things and persons
Their time, their rhythm and their place, their opportunities and their
lifespan:

Grant me a pure and peaceful wisdom
To savour every moment of the time you give to me,
That I may live to the full and glorify you more and more, now and for ever.
Amen.

(Howard Peskett)

*   There are two words for time in the New Testament. *chronos* refers to chronological, measured time—clock and diary time. *kairos* is the time Jesus declares—'*now is the time.*' The word means 'season,' 'special moment,' 'fitting opportunity.'

4

The Search for Belonging

'And God said, it is *not good* for *adam* to be alone.' (Genesis 2.18)

Seeing
Look again at the sculpture for a while.

Adam is alone with God in this picture. It looks a solitary becoming, in God's presence.

In the second creation story (Gen 2.4–3.24) we are told that he was lonely in the Garden (2.18). This is not the estrangement and loneliness that is due to sin. That comes later in the story. This is a loneliness that is part of the original goodness of Creation.

Connecting
In the first creation story *adam* is the last living creature to be made—the crown and climax of God's creating work. Here *adam* is first and he is alone. There follows a wonderfully playful scene where God directs the vast variety of other creeping, crawling, walking and flying creatures towards *adam* 'to see what he would call them' (Genesis 2.18–19). Companionship and community are not tailor-made for *adam*. He has to go out and make relationships.

Reflecting
The only thing that was *not* good in the Garden of Eden was that *adam* was alone. Incompleteness—being unfinished—was part of the original blessing and goodness of creation. And this involves a search for belonging, identity and relationship in creation. Note that this is not a need that can God fulfil. When one man found courage to share, in a Christian discussion group, how lonely he often felt he was told 'but Jesus is your friend.' And he replied, 'But Jesus doesn't play golf!'

Even in the closest friendships, which echo *adam's* cry of joyful recognition—'at last!'—when he meets Eve, there can be times of painful isolation and struggle to communicate.

It can often be in company that we can feel most alone. So relationships, friendships and marriage are not *solutions* to loneliness. They are contexts in which we experience ourselves in all our incompleteness. They are gifts of God in a search for wholeness and fellowship that we all share. We become through them.

Writing from a lifetime's experience living in Christian communities, Jean Vanier observes:

Community can appear to be a marvellously welcoming and sharing place. But in another way, community is a terrible place. It is the place where our limitations and our egoism are revealed to us. When we begin to live full-time with others, we discover our poverty and our weaknesses, our inability to get on with people, our mental and emotional blocks, our affective and sexual disturbances, our seemingly insatiable desires, our frustrations and jealousies, our hatred and our wish to destroy. While we were alone, we could believe we loved everyone.

Not only are *we* unfinished. So are those around us. It is not necessarily the sin and selfishness of others that makes human relationships so difficult. It is just that we are so *different* from each other! We all have different personalities, interests, hopes and expectations.

By placing the loneliness of *adam* in the original goodness of creation this story is insisting there is a gift to be found here.

One thing loneliness does teach us after all, is the falsity of imagining that we possess any wholeness ourselves. Loneliness uncovers for us the tedium and poverty of our own private worlds; it lays bare what has been called the 'raw surface' of our need for others and our need for communication. I am not a whole person, and there is no such thing as a whole person—in the sense of a wholeness sufficient in and to itself.

(Rowan Williams)

Part of the task in our maturing is the willingness to negotiate between our cherished ideals and the actual reality of what is given. This life is what is given while we were hoping for another. Life, in that sense, is a continuing pilgrimage of reconciliation. This is not necessarily because life has gone wrong. We only grow into our humanity when we are prepared to reach out, to call by name and enter into a creation that is continually, joyfully, painfully and infuriatingly *different* from ourselves!

Responding

Can you identify with the solitary figure of *adam*? Where do you 'belong'? What is 'not good' about your own belonging and relating at present? Can you give it a name?

If you recognize yourself in some of the reflections above, is there an act of reconciliation or meeting you need to make in some way—perhaps a conversation, a letter, an action or a prayer?

'If we come into community without knowing that the reason we come is to discover the mystery of forgiveness, we will soon be disappointed.' (Jean Vanier)

Can you draw loneliness? What colour is it? Does it have a shape? Try using paint, charcoal or clay to express your response to the aloneness of adam.

A Prayer of Reconciliation to Life
It may help to use this prayer after careful reflection on what or who is being forgiven and why. Some may find it helpful to use a candle as a symbol of seeking new life through this prayer.

'We must forgive earth for not being heaven.' (Neville Ward)

I forgive	earth for not being heaven
	time for not being eternity
	faith for not being certainty
	dust for not being glory
I forgive	beginnings for not being endings
	questions for not being answers
	confusion for not being understanding
	darkness for not being light
I forgive	mind for not being heart
	man for not being woman
	passion for not being compassion
	conflict for not being peace
	evil for not being good
	you for not being me
I forgive	and holding a mirror to the prayer
	I start again

I forgive forgiveness never ending.

(David Runcorn)

5

The Wound of Becoming

'Then the Lord God *formed adam* from the dust of the ground' (Genesis 2.7)

Seeing
Start by looking at the sculpture. How has your 'seeing' of this sculpture changed through these meditations?

As I look at this sculpture I want to ask, 'What was *adam's* experience of being created?' Here we may share different impressions. It may be the effect of weathering and the shadow across *adam's* face but he seems exhausted with the effort of being created. He could be in pain. He looks disorientated. Here is the crowning high point of God's creation, slumped against the divine lap and clutching at God's knee as if in danger of sliding back into the dust of the earth.

What does it all take out of him? Will he make it?

Connecting
'Life is difficult' was the first sentence of the best selling book *The Road Less Travelled*, by Scott Peck. I remember how liberated I felt when I first read those words. It was all right to feel like that! This is not only the testimony of those in despair. Ask explorers and pioneers. That life is difficult is all the challenge they need! But there are times when the demand and cost of entering life even with God, is just too much. The haunting end to Psalm 39 is one example. 'O Lord, what do I wait for? My hope is in you...do not hide your face at my tears. Turn your gaze away from me, that I may smile again, before I depart and am no more' (Ps 39.7, 12–13). St Paul knew of times when...'we were so utterly, unbearably crushed that we despaired of life itself...' (2 Cor 1.8).

Our creation, as much as our re-creation, will take us to our limits and at times we may be unsure if we can give or take any more.

Reflecting
People seeing this sculpture for the first time tend to assume it is a picture of Jesus forgiving a sinner—or perhaps the father welcoming home his prodigal son. It comes as some surprise that the scene is actually from the original goodness of creation. It does not look like good news—at least not yet.

The ambiguity may have been intentional on the part of the sculptor. Perhaps creation and re-creation make very similar demands on us. Both are costly. The same person who said, 'I have come that they may have life, and have it abundantly,' (John 10.10) also said, 'it is a narrow gate and a hard road that leads to life—and those who find it are few' (Matt 7.13–14).

Out of a right concern to expose the terrible effect of sin, there has always been a temptation to imagine what life was like in that innocent Paradise. The story-teller in Genesis carefully avoids any such speculation. The action quickly moves to the 'Fall' and so to the world that every reader recognizes as a present reality (though we may have different ways of explaining what has happened). But the pictures of this 'perfect' Garden in children's Bible books hardly suggest a place of any excitement or challenge. Even without the terrible fact and consequence of the entry of sin into the world, it is hard to imagine a world in which there is a vocation to explore, to grow, to make choices and to enter into relationship with all that is made—without there being an experience of struggle, or pain and loss.

So it may be that we can only receive this invitation to be becomers as a wound—a wound of grace. Becoming disables us. It has to. Real becoming con-tradicts so much of what life teaches us is necessary (and Christian ideals of disci-pleship are part of all this). All our repeated projects, designed to meet our need to feel finished and in control, must be tripped up.

It is a severe but loving mercy that reminds us we remain unfinished.

Not for nothing has this experience been described as 'the harrowing opera-tion of conversion' (Charles Williams). In the process of ageing, becoming is be-ing completed through diminishment and eventual surrender.

There is a sense in which every minister of the gospel is diminished by their ministry. If they have any self-knowledge at all, their ministry makes them less confident in themselves, less assured, less doctrinaire and therefore less secure. They become more aware of the dark places in their own lives and in the lives of others. Anyone who has been long in the ministry will know the time when they have to say 'I stumble, where once I firmly trod.'

(Stuart Blanch)

Responding

Imagine a cartoon bubble drawn out of *adam's* mouth. What is he saying as he slumps against God's lap?

What do *you* want to say?

What is your experience of the gift and/or wound of becoming?

How does this sound?

A weary and wounded disciple, feeling deeply the elusiveness of life:
'When will it all be finished? How long will it all take?'
God replies, with a warm smile—'As long as you like.'

For those praying out of pain and personal darkness, this thought, in the light of the sculpture:

Is my gloom, after all, Shade of His hand outstretched caressingly?
(Francis Thompson, *The Hound of Heaven*)

19

May our only wounds be these:
> The wound that we cannot avoid
> Because we belong to one another,
> And feel and hear the murmur of the world's pain;
> The wound of a sense of compassion for others;
> The wound of a sense of longing for God,
> The Source of Life and Love
> deep within us and far beyond us.

(Jim Cotter)

6

The Cost of Creating

'And God *breathed* into his nostrils and he became a *living being*' (Gen 2.7)

Seeing
Look again, for a while, at the picture of this sculpture.
Remember the time God took to look at every stage of his creation.

Have you found the cross in this picture?
It is just behind the head of God.
What is the cross doing in the story of creation?

Look again.

Connecting
What does it cost God to make the world? At first glance the smooth, untroubled features of God in this sculpture makes creating look quite effortless. The story suggests the same. 'God spoke...and it was done!' A flick of divine fingers and here we are! And this is the way the creation story in Genesis is usually told.

But the cross behind his head hints at a cost to it all in a way not yet made apparent.

The New Testament teaches us that Jesus reveals the unseen God. 'Christ is the exact likeness of the unseen God' (Col 1.15). Jesus himself said, 'Whoever has seen me has seen the Father' (John 14.9). We are accustomed to contemplating Jesus in the work of salvation as redemption, freeing us from sin. But how does our awareness of Jesus as the image of God change our understanding of the work of creation?

How does a Christlike God create and sustain the world?

Reflecting

A key verse for understanding this is Philippians 2.6, where Christ Jesus, *'though he was in the form of God….emptied himself* [the Greek word is *kenosis*], *taking the form of a slave, being born in human likeness.'* If this is how God rescues us, it is first of all the way he creates. He pours his whole self into what he has made.

In his book *Love's Endeavour, Love's Expense*, W H Vanstone illustrates this with a story. A medical student tells of how he observed a leading surgeon performing an eye operation. The task was so delicate that there was no margin for error. The outcome was a triumph. But after seven hours intense, uninterrupted concentration, the surgeon was so exhausted and spent that he had to be led from the operating theatre by the hand, like a 'blind man, or a little child.' Vanstone concludes, 'Always, for the richness of the creation, God is made poor, and for its fullness God is made empty.'

Instead of a creation sustained by effortless divine power, we are being asked to contemplate something very different. The first words God speaks in the Bible are 'Let there be.' He does not decree 'I will have.' They carry a sense of gracious invitation—of possibility not prescription. And this is underlined by how much God leaves *adam* to choose and explore the possibilities of life.

If the cross reveals God's creating, as well as his redeeming, then perhaps

> the activity of God in creation must be precarious. It proceeds with no assured programme. Its progress, like every progress of love, must be an angular progress—in which each step is a precarious step into an unknown…Creation is 'safe' not because it moves by programming towards a predetermined goal but because the same loving creativity is ever exercised upon it. (Vanstone)

So the love that overshadows *adam* in this picture of creating is a costly, utterly self-giving love. It is crucified love that brings this world into being.

Responding

This sculpture is not questioning whether God is all powerful. But by placing the cross in the Garden of Eden, it does ask us to consider, in the light of Christ, how God uses and expresses his power. Rather 'God is Christlike and in him is no *un*Christlikeness' (A M Ramsey).

This may be a new way of thinking about God the Creator. Is it comforting? Is it disturbing? Might it change the way you picture or pray or appreciate your relationship with God?

This takes us back to the sculpture again with an unexpected question. Where, after all, is God in this picture? Which one is the image of God? The apparently serene, compassionate creator? Or the figure looking exhausted and incomplete beneath? This is a God who shares our becoming one with us, by sharing our flesh and nature.

And if you were in this picture—which figure would you be? The strong caring enabler? Or the vulnerable, dependent, becomer? It may not be the same as the figure that other people require you to be.

God and Our Prayers

'There is a deeply humbling mutual exchange, a mutual *kenosis* [emptying], in all our dealings with God. Any costly generosity towards him on our part draws out of him our prodigal Father, a costly graciousness and an overwhelming mercy far in excess of what is "necessary."

In my own experience, after what I thought was a tired hour's failure to pray and focus on the cross, and I felt I wanted to say "thank you for your wounds," he said "thank you for yours." To my desire to thank him for everything, I sensed his "thank *you* for everything." To my, "thank you for being so patient with me," I felt him say "thank *you* for being so patient." Thank you for letting go of what you do not need.

The waiting, the excruciating longing, the holding on against hope is all mutual.

In the darkness, even the very things that have stymied us become the means by which we are drawn back to Christ...'

(Philip Seddon)

Is there anything you want to say to God at the end of this meditation?

7

Blessing and Hallowing

'And on the seventh day he *rested* from all the work he had done.' (Gen 2.2)

Seeing
Start by just looking at the sculpture again.
This scene in the sculpture is very restful. It may be due to the weathering over the years, but God's eyes seem to be shut. His hands are quietly poised—not frozen in mid action.

adam is resting against God's lap, his hand clutching God's knee. There is a companionable silence between them. At some point the work of creating will resume, but for now let there be quiet and stillness and time to restore strength.

Connecting
Creation was not completed when the physical tasks were finished on the sixth day. The story clearly says it was 'on the seventh day God finished the work that he had done...So God blessed the seventh day and hallowed it, because on it God rested...' (Genesis 2.2–3). The word 'rest' is easily misunderstood here. This is not the rest at the end of an exhausting week's work. It is the celebration of something *begun*. This is actually the first full day of creation. In this world you rest before work and not after. Sabbath blessing is received and entered as free gift—not a reward for effort or achievement.

Reflecting
The sabbath expresses God's fullest intention and longing for a creation at home and alive in the fullness of his presence and sustaining love.

There is a discipline of celebration here that Christian lifestyle must be careful to guard and honour. Not for nothing did the Old Testament prophets regard the neglect of the sabbath as something terrible in the life of God's people. It is the clearest symptom of a world that has lost faith and trust in God.

Faced with the idolizing of urgency, efficiency, problem-solving, successful achievement, money, practicality, crisis management and all those other compulsions that never let us take time off with a good conscience, the sabbath is...the secret of resistance. (David Ford)
The 'rest' in the sculpture is not our final rest in God's kingdom—the final fulfilment of all God's intention. Our sabbaths now anticipate, remind and prepare us for the great 'Eighth Day' as it is sometimes called.

Creation only exists because God takes pleasure in it; he has no need to create. In that sense creation is pointless, useless in and of itself! 'This world has no reason or basis to live except to live in the celebration of God's gracious being.' The vision of the seventh day in the creation story is closer to playing than working!

Responding

The seventh day of creation is a celebration and rest in the fullness of all that has been given life. Are there ways this final time of meditation might capture the spirit of this day? Perhaps a glass of wine, or cake—music or even dance?

We will each want to express different things—and will choose different ways to express them. That too is part of the gift of our humanity and the gift of community.

O Lord, my heart is not lifted up, My eyes are not raised too high;
I do not occupy myself with great matters or things that are too hard for me.
But I still my soul and make it quiet.
Like a child upon its mother's breast; my soul is quieted within me.
O Israel, hope in the Lord from this time forth and for evermore.

Psalm 131

What place does sabbath celebration have in your life?
What place does it have in the life of the community you belong to?
When did you last play as a celebration of sabbath with God?
Can you plan in your diary now a time when you will do this?
What would that time include? Would it help to plan it with others?

'And God saw *all* that he had made...and it was very good'

Take time to review the words, thoughts, feelings, pictures, forms and objects that have been part of your exploring and praying the creation story.

Are there particular insights, challenges or questions that you could still explore? What activity action might help you to do this?

Taking Leave

Are there words you wish to speak to *adam* or to God as this seven fold meditation comes to an end?

Closing Blessing
The Father,
bending down from heaven,
Come cradle the child within you,
Cradle the child within you

Jesus, born of Mary
Whose heart was pierced,
Come heal the wounds within you,
Heal the wounds within you.

The Spirit, poured out for Sabbath play,
Come release new life within you,
Release new life within you.
Amen